For ....

From ....

Date ....

HUNDREDS OF
Awesome Quotes

DAD

ABOUT THE GUY WHO
DOES IT ALL

ADAMS MEDIA
NEW YORK   LONDON   TORONTO   SYDNEY   NEW DELHI

Adams Media
An Imprint of Simon & Schuster, Inc.
57 Littlefield Street
Avon, Massachusetts 02322

First Adams Media trade paperback edition APRIL 2017

ADAMS MEDIA and colophon are trademarks of Simon and Schuster.

For information about special discounts for bulk purchases, please contact Simon & Schuster Special Sales at 1-866-506-1949 or business@simonandschuster.com.

The Simon & Schuster Speakers Bureau can bring authors to your live event. For more information or to book an event contact the Simon & Schuster Speakers Bureau at 1-866-248-3049 or visit our website at www.simonspeakers.com.

Interior design by Colleen Cunningham

Manufactured in the United States of America

10 9 8 7 6 5 4 3 2 1

Library of Congress Cataloging-in-Publication Data has been applied for.

ISBN 978-1-5072-0299-9
ISBN 978-1-5072-0300-2 (ebook)

Contains material adapted from the following title published by Adams Media, an Imprint of Simon & Schuster, Inc.: *All about Dad*, edited by Dahlia Porter and Gabriel Cervantes, copyright © 2007, ISBN 978-1-59869-142-9.

Introduction

The bond between a father and his child is special and sacred. It takes great strength and selflessness to be a good father; to love unconditionally and without hesitation. *DAD* captures the joys—and the occasional frustrations—of fatherhood, with contributions from actors to athletes and presidents to poets.

Take a break from the blissful chaos of family life to read these poignant, funny, and insightful looks at fatherhood. From the elegant words of ancient scholars to Louis C.K.'s brutally honest assessment of his parenting skills, these quotes are sure to make you smile and remember: You are appreciated; you are admired; you are loved.

To a young boy, a father is a giant from whose shoulders you can see forever.

PERRY GARFINKEL, JOURNALIST

Every father bears a fundamental obligation to do right by their children.

BARACK OBAMA, 44TH PRESIDENT OF THE UNITED STATES

My dad believed in me, even when I didn't. He always knew I could do this.

TAYLOR SWIFT, MUSICIAN

Blessed indeed is the man who hears many gentle voices call him father!

LYDIA MARIA CHILD, WOMEN'S RIGHTS ACTIVIST

My father was the role model
I looked up to. My dad was an
entertainer, too. I patterned my
life after him. He wanted me to
do better than he did. He never
sold a record in his life, but to me,
he was still a rock star.

TRACY MORGAN, COMEDIAN

The last few weeks for me have been a very different emotional experience, something I never thought I would feel myself. And I find, again it's only been a short period, but a lot of things affect me differently now.

⊳ PRINCE WILLIAM, DUKE OF CAMBRIDGE ◁

"Father" is the noblest title a man can be given.

⊳ ROBERT L. BACKMAN, GENERAL AUTHORITY OF THE CHURCH OF JESUS CHRIST OF LATTER-DAY SAINTS ◁

My father always told me, "Find a job you love and you'll never have to work a day in your life."

JIM FOX, PROFESSIONAL HOCKEY PLAYER

She has me so far wrapped around her finger, it's dumb. She says "Dada" and I will walk through a cement wall to get to her. It's crazy. . . . I love it. I truly worship that kid.

RYAN REYNOLDS, ACTOR

Fatherhood is the single most creative, complicated, fulfilling, frustrating, engrossing, enriching, depleting endeavor of a man's adult life.

KYLE D. PRUETT,
PROFESSOR OF CHILD PSYCHIATRY

It sounds so clichéd, but I never knew that life could be this fun and this great.

◖ RYAN GOSLING, ACTOR ◗

He that will have his son have respect for him and his orders, must himself have a great reverence for his son.

◖ JOHN LOCKE, ENGLISH PHILOSOPHER ◗

My Father taught me how to be a man—and not by instilling in me a sense of machismo or an agenda of dominance. He taught me that a real man doesn't take, he gives; he doesn't use force, he uses logic; doesn't play the role of trouble-maker, but rather, trouble-shooter; and most importantly, a real man is defined by what's in his heart, not his pants.

KEVIN SMITH, ACTOR AND DIRECTOR

There are a couple of pictures of the two of us that are of great sentimental value. In one, he's holding a bat in his left hand and has me comfortably balanced on his right shoulder. Some of the photos may be faded, but the memories of the happy times we spent together will always remain sharp and clear in my mind.

DOROTHY RUTH PICONE, DAUGHTER OF BABE RUTH

What I've realized is that life doesn't count for much unless you're willing to do your small part to leave our children—all of our children—a better world. Even if it's difficult. . . . That is our ultimate responsibility as fathers and parents. We try. We hope.

BARACK OBAMA, 44TH PRESIDENT OF THE UNITED STATES

Once you've been launched into parenthood, you'll need all your best skills, self-control, good judgment and patience. But at the same time there is nothing like the thrill and exhilaration that come from watching that bright, cheerful, inquisitive, creative, eccentric and even goofy child you have raised flourish and shine. That's what keeps you going, and what, in the end, makes it all worthwhile.

LAWRENCE BALTER, PSYCHOLOGIST

The father who does not teach his son his duties is equally guilty with the son who neglects them.

CONFUCIUS, PHILOSOPHER

Dad gave me two pieces of advice. One was "No matter how good you think you are, there are people better than you." But he was an optimist too; his other advice: "Never worry about rejection. Every day is a new beginning."

JOHN RITTER, ACTOR

It's legitimately the *greatest* thing ever. . . . It just makes me wanna be *better*.

ASHTON KUTCHER, ACTOR

Sometimes the poorest man leaves
his children the richest inheritance.

⊳ RUTH E. RENKEL, WRITER ⊲

In my career there's many things I've won and many
things I've achieved. But my greatest achievement
is my family. What matters is being a good father
and a good husband—just being connected to family
as much as possible. Being a dad is more important
than football, more important than anything. I adore
children. I love the fact our children are part of both
of us. It's one of the most amazing things ever.

⊳ DAVID BECKHAM, PROFESSIONAL SOCCER PLAYER ⊲

His father watched him across
the gulf of years and pathos
which always must divide
a father from his son.

J.P. MARQUAND, WRITER

Being a father is certainly a task . . . but the best one that I could ever ask for. Being home, being with the family—that's what it's about.

CHRIS HEMSWORTH, ACTOR

There is a mirror that is held up to me now. You have someone watching you. You have to lead by example.

⊷ JOHN KRASINSKI, ACTOR ⊶

The time not to become a father is eighteen years before a world war.

⊷ E.B. WHITE, WRITER ⊶

The toughest part of parenthood has nothing to do with putting food on the table, clothes in the closet, or tuition money in the bank. The toughest part of parenthood is never knowing if you're doing the right thing.

D.L. STEWART, NEWSPAPER COLUMNIST

Sons have always a rebellious wish to be disillusioned by that which charmed their fathers.

ALDOUS HUXLEY, WRITER

A father carries pictures where his money used to be.

❧ ANONYMOUS ❧

The only way I can describe [fatherhood]—it sounds stupid, but—at the end of *How the Grinch Stole Christmas*, you know how his heart grows, like, five times its size? Everything is full; it's just full all the time.

❧ MATT DAMON, ACTOR ❧

I didn't think it was going to be this fun. But everything just gets heightened when you have a baby. The volume gets turned up on life. I never knew I could be this happy, and that's the truth.

⊳ JIMMY FALLON, COMEDIAN ⊲

It is a great moment in life when a father sees a son grow taller than he or reach farther.

⊳ RICHARD L. EVANS, MEMBER OF THE QUORUM OF THE TWELVE APOSTLES OF THE CHURCH OF JESUS CHRIST OF LATTER-DAY SAINTS ⊲

I always tell my kids, "You know what? The biggest thing you can have in life is *passion*."

What was silent in the father speaks in
the son; and often I found in the son
the unveiled secret of the father.

FRIEDRICH NIETZSCHE, GERMAN PHILOSOPHER

My dad kept giving me
"love pats." Love pats are soft
punches of encouragement that
are administered on the knee,
shoulder, and arm.

STEPHEN CHBOSKY, WRITER

I know that I will never find my father in any other man who comes into my life, because it is a void that can only be filled by him.

Three stages in a parent's life: nutrition, dentition, tuition.

[Fatherhood is] the greatest thing that could ever happen. You can't explain it until it happens—it's like telling somebody what water feels like before they've ever swam in it.

◈ MICHAEL BUBLÉ, MUSICIAN ◈

A man's desire for a son is usually nothing but the wish to duplicate himself in order that such a remarkable pattern may not be lost to the world.

◈ HELEN ROWLAND, WRITER ◈

[Fatherhood taught me] heavy lessons about simplicity and unconditional love. I don't want to sound cliché—another father talking about unconditional love—but man, that's the way it is. You hear it all the time, but when you feel this other branch of love getting stronger and stronger every day, it's just amazing.

🔊 RICKY MARTIN, MUSICIAN 🔊

All we have of freedom—all we use or know—
This our fathers bought for us, long and long ago.

RUDYARD KIPLING, WRITER

Every day, you are teaching your children what it means to be a father.

LARRY M. GIBSON, FIRST COUNSELOR IN THE
YOUNG MEN GENERAL PRESIDENCY OF THE
CHURCH OF JESUS CHRIST OF LATTER-DAY SAINTS

If you are a parent, it helps if you are a grownup.

▷ EDA J. LESHAN, WRITER ◁

I've always followed my father's advice: he told me, first to always keep my word and, second, to never insult anybody unintentionally. If I insult you, you can be goddamn sure I intend to. And, third, he told me not to go around looking for trouble.

▷ JOHN WAYNE, ACTOR ◁

No matter what drama I deal with at work, *when I get home* and hear them scream, "Daddy!" I forget whatever it was I was stressed about.

MARIO LOPEZ, ACTOR

For a boy to reach adulthood feeling that he knows his father, his father must allow his emotions to be visible—hardly an easy task when most males grow up being either subtly or openly taught that this is not acceptable behavior. A father must teach his son that masculinity and feelings can go hand in hand.

KYLE D. PRUETT, PROFESSOR OF CHILD PSYCHIATRY

When you have kids, you see life through different eyes. You feel love more deeply and are maybe a little more compassionate.

DAVE GROHL, MUSICIAN

Until you have a son of your own . . .
you will never know the joy, the love
beyond feeling that resonates in the heart
of a father as he looks upon his son.

❧ KENT NERBURN, WRITER ❧

The mark of a good parent is that he can have fun while being one.

❧ MARCELENE COX, WRITER ❧

I talk and talk and talk,
and I haven't taught people in
50 years what my father taught
by example in one week.

MARIO CUOMO, POLITICIAN

As fathers, we need to be involved in
our children's lives not just when it's convenient
or easy, and not just when they're doing well—
but when it's difficult and thankless, and they're
struggling. That is when they need us most.

BARACK OBAMA, 44TH PRESIDENT OF THE UNITED STATES

I try to teach my children there are going to be obstacles. Someone may not like you just because they don't like themselves. But, don't you get bogged down.

⊳ DENZEL WASHINGTON, ACTOR ⊲

Let children know you are human.
It's important for children to see that parents
are human and make mistakes. When you're sorry
about something you've said or done, apologize!
It is best when parents apologize in a manner that
is straightforward and sincere.

SAF LERMAN, WRITER

My daddy was my hero.
He was always there for me when
I needed him. But most of all he was fun.

BINDI IRWIN, ACTRESS AND TELEVISION PERSONALITY

To maintain a joyful family requires much from both the parents and the children. Each member of the family has to become, in a special way, the servant of the others.

POPE JOHN PAUL II

My heart is happy, my mind is free, I had a father who talked with me.

HILDA BIGELOW, WRITER

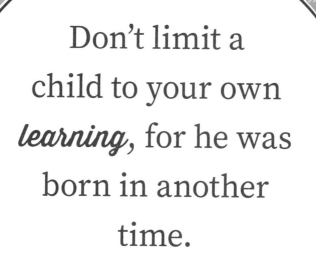

Don't limit a child to your own *learning*, for he was born in another time.

🎺 JEWISH PROVERB 🎺

My father always told me: You have the rest of your life to figure out what you want to do with the rest of your life.

JOHN BEILENSON, BUSINESSMAN

A father's duty is to make his home a place of happiness and joy.

EZRA TAFT BENSON, 13TH PRESIDENT OF THE CHURCH OF JESUS CHRIST OF LATTER-DAY SAINTS

For many of us, our fathers show us by the example they set the kind of people they want us to become. Whether biological, foster, or adoptive, they teach us through the encouragement they give, the questions they answer, the limits they set, and the strength they show in the face of difficulty and hardship.

BARACK OBAMA, 44TH PRESIDENT OF THE UNITED STATES

[My father] passed on to me to treat others the way you want to be treated. I think that's why I'd like to think the way I carry myself and do my business and do things is because of my mom and dad and the way they raised me. It's one of those things I'm trying to pass on to my kids.

MARK BUEHRLE, PROFESSIONAL BASEBALL PLAYER

The most important thing that parents can teach their children is how to get along without them.

FRANK A. CLARK, WRITER

Everything I thought I'd hate about having children—the crying, the screaming—nothing fazes me. I love it all and it's relaxed me. It's just so wonderful to have someone in the house like a child to turn your attention to. It's not about you anymore, it's about this lovely little human being.

ELTON JOHN, MUSICIAN

[Parenting] is hit or miss. And it's experimental. So for me, it's a deep uncertainty, that I carry around, with my kids. I just try to teach them everything that I know and love them as hard as I can love them. And hope for the best.

WILL SMITH, ACTOR

When I think of my father, the memories that bubble to the surface are not policy or politics. They are the man who opened a child's imagination, who taught her to be a good horsewoman and to always get back on when I fell off.

PATTI DAVIS, DAUGHTER OF RONALD REAGAN

A wise father teaches skills. Courage. Concentration on the job in hand. Self-discipline. Encourages enthusiasm. A spirit of enquiry. Gentleness. Kindliness. Patience. Courtesy. And love.

PAM BROWN, WRITER

The most important lesson
I learned from my father is to be actively
involved in your child's life. My dad was
not the most communicative, nurturing,
or friendliest person around. But he
took an interest in what I did,
and gave me endless support.

TONY HAWK, PROFESSIONAL SKATEBOARDER

I used to feel that all I ever
did was take from my father:
"Dad, my heater's not working."
"Dad, I need help building the shed."
"Dad, can you lend me money for
a car?" Now he has a computer.
Things are evening up quickly.

⊳ DEN SCHLAF, WRITER ⊲

The greatest mark of a father is how he treats his children when no one is looking.

⊨ DAN PEARCE, WRITER ⊨

A boy needs a father to show him how to be in the world. He needs to be given swagger, taught how to read a map so that he can recognize the roads that lead to life and the paths that lead to death, how to know what love requires, and where to find steel in the heart when life makes demands on us that are greater than we think we can endure.

⊨ IAN MORGAN CRON, WRITER ⊨

When I come home, my daughter will run to the door and give me a big hug, and everything that's happened that day just melts away.

🕊 HUGH JACKMAN, ACTOR 🕊

Rich men's sons are seldom rich men's fathers.

🕊 HERBERT KAUFMAN, WRITER 🕊

My dad always said, "Don't worry what people think, because you can't change it."

⚑ DAISY DONOVAN, TELEVISION PRESENTER AND ACTRESS ⚑

My father taught me that the only way you can make good at anything is to practice, and then practice some more.

⚑ PETE ROSE, PROFESSIONAL BASEBALL PLAYER ⚑

My father was very strong. I don't agree with a lot of the ways he brought me up. I don't agree with a lot of his values, but he did have a lot of integrity, and if he told us not to do something, he didn't do it either.

◈ MADONNA, MUSICIAN ◈

When a father gives his daughter an emotional visa to strike out on her own, he is always with her. Such a daughter has her encouraging, understanding daddy in her head, cheering her on—not simply as a woman but as a whole, unique human being with unlimited possibilities.

⪢ VICTORIA SECUNDA, WRITER ⪡

My father was my teacher. But most importantly he was a great dad.

⪢ BEAU BRIDGES, ACTOR ⪡

Being a father,
being a friend,
those are the
things that make
me feel *successful*.

WILLIAM HURT, ACTOR

Dads are like chocolate chip cookies; they may have chips or be totally nutty, but they are sweet and make the world a better place, especially for their children.

HILLARY LYTLE, WRITER

The other night, I was walking down the stairs behind one of my daughters—I have three, and one son, ages eight to sixteen. I was tired, and she was goofing around, you know, like kids do, doing all this stupid stuff on the stairs. And I was thinking, "Please just go down the stairs and let's get you to bed. It's after your bedtime. I've had enough for one day." And then I sort of caught myself. I snapped out of it. I was like, "Dude, you should be dancing down the stairs behind her!"

⮞ FOREST WHITAKER, ACTOR ⮜

I don't expect the human race to progress in too many areas. However, having a child with an ear infection makes one hugely grateful for antibiotics.

❦ DAVID BOWIE, MUSICIAN ❦

When it comes to parenthood everyone thinks they will be terrible at it. We don't think we have it in us. Then you find out that you do, which truly is a miracle in life.

❦ DANIEL DAY-LEWIS, ACTOR ❦

My dad, like any coach, has always stressed the fundamentals. He taught me responsibility, accountability, and the importance of hard work.

STEVE YOUNG, PROFESSIONAL FOOTBALL PLAYER

I think the best thing to try
to do is allow your daughter
or your son to know that they
can come to you for anything.
If you can break down
that wall so they don't feel
embarrassed by telling you
things, that's half the battle.

JAMIE FOXX, ACTOR

I've got incredible pride for my family.
I've absolutely fallen into that cliché of a dad who
could just happily talk about my daughter endlessly.

⊳ CHRISTIAN BALE, ACTOR ⊲

Many a man wishes he were
strong enough to tear a telephone
book in half, especially if he has
a teenage daughter.

⊳ GUY LOMBARDO, MUSICIAN ⊲

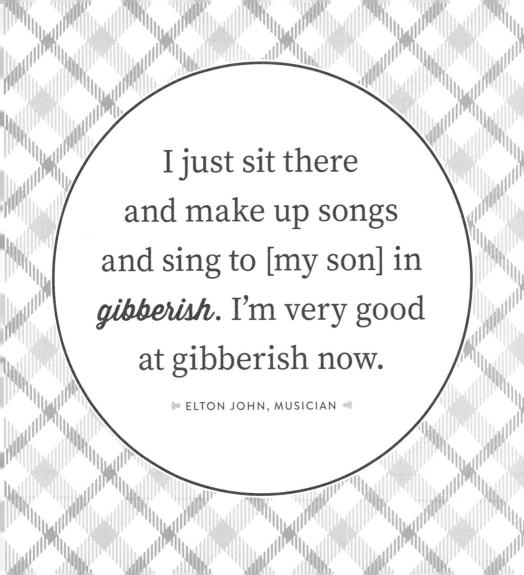

I just sit there
and make up songs
and sing to [my son] in
gibberish. I'm very good
at gibberish now.

ELTON JOHN, MUSICIAN

A wedding is for daughters and fathers. The mothers all dress up, trying to look like young women. But a wedding is for a father and daughter. They stop being married to each other on that day.

🕊 SARAH RUHL, WRITER 🕊

During the sole argument we had when [Chelsea] was in high school, the subject of which I don't even remember, I looked at her and said, "As long as you're in this house, being president is my second most important job."

🕊 BILL CLINTON, 42ND PRESIDENT OF THE UNITED STATES 🕊

I remember being at a point below his knees and looking up past the vast length of him. He was six foot three; his voice was big. He was devastatingly attractive— even to his daughter as a child. . . . His voice was so beautiful, so enveloping. He was just bigger and better than anyone else.

ANJELICA HUSTON, ACTRESS

There is something like a line of gold thread running through the man's words when he talks to his daughter, and gradually over the years it gets to be long enough for you to pick up in your hands and weave into a cloth that feels like love itself.

⮞ JOHN GREGORY BROWN, WRITER ⮜

My dad was my hero. And I got my personality from my mother.

⮞ MAGIC JOHNSON, PROFESSIONAL BASKETBALL PLAYER ⮜

There should be a children's song:
"If you're happy and you know it, keep it to
yourself and let your dad sleep."

🔊 JIM GAFFIGAN, COMEDIAN 🔊

There is magic in the moment, for when I open my
eyes and see my sons in the place where my father
once sat, I feel an invisible bond between our three
generations, an anchor of loyalty linking my sons
to be the grandfather whose face they never saw
but whose person they have already come to know
through this most timeless of all sports, baseball.

🔊 DORIS KEARNS GOODWIN, WRITER 🔊

I can do one of two things. I can be president of the United States, or I can control Alice. I cannot possibly do both.

☞ THEODORE ROOSEVELT, 26TH PRESIDENT OF THE UNITED STATES ☜

I found out that I'm a pretty bad father. I make a lot of mistakes and I don't know what I'm doing. But my kids love me. Go figure.

☞ LOUIS C.K., COMEDIAN ☜

I want my son to wear a helmet 24 hours a day.
If it was socially acceptable I'd be the first
one to have my kid in a full helmet and
like a cage across his face mask.

WILL ARNETT, ACTOR

Never fret for an only son, the idea
of failure will never occur to him.

GEORGE BERNARD SHAW, WRITER

It is not flesh and blood but the *heart* which makes us fathers and sons.

FRIEDRICH VON SCHILLER, GERMAN WRITER AND PHILOSOPHER

I have found the best way to give advice to your children is to find out what they want and then advise them to do it.

The older I get, the smarter my father seems to get.

Watching your daughter being collected by her date feels like handing over a $1 million Stradivarius to a gorilla.

🕊 JIM BISHOP, WRITER 🕊

When someone who knew my father says I'm like him, I feel flattered. He was a shy, undemonstrative man, but good natured with a great, whimsical sense of humor.

🕊 PAUL NEWMAN, ACTOR 🕊

My dad was always there for me and my brother, and I want my kids to have the same kind of dad—a dad they will remember. Being a dad is the most important thing in my life.

◀ KEVIN COSTNER, ACTOR ▶

When I was a boy of fourteen, my father was so ignorant I could hardly stand to have the old man around. But when I got to be twenty-one, I was astonished at how much the old man had learned in seven years.

⊳ MARK TWAIN, WRITER ⊲

Fatherhood is great because you can ruin someone from scratch.

⊳ JON STEWART, COMEDIAN ⊲

**I'll never forget the moment I became
a dad. It's hard to describe—that level of
responsibility, the desire to give such joy,
the clarity: Nothing is more important than this.**

🕊 TOM CRUISE, ACTOR 🕊

I'm probably the most uncool guy that
[my daughters] know—as far as they are
concerned anyway—'cause I'm Dad. I mean
dads just aren't cool—especially when
I dance! They don't want me to dance.

🕊 TIM MCGRAW, MUSICIAN 🕊

I believe that what we become depends on what our fathers teach us at odd moments, when they aren't trying to teach us. We are formed by little scraps of wisdom.

⊱ UMBERTO ECO, WRITER ⊰

A man knows he is growing old because he begins to look like his father.

⊱ GABRIEL GARCÍA MÁRQUEZ, WRITER ⊰

It was my father
who taught me to value
myself. He told me that I was
uncommonly beautiful and
that I was the most precious
thing in his life.

DAWN FRENCH, ACTRESS

The heart of a father is the masterpiece of nature.

Having children is like living in a frat house—nobody sleeps, everything's broken, and there's a lot of throwing up.

By the time a man realizes that maybe his father was right, he usually has a son who thinks he's wrong.

CHARLES WADSWORTH, MUSICIAN

Before I got married I had six theories about raising children; now, I have six children and no theories.

JOHN WILMOT, WRITER

My greatest memories as a kid were playing sports
with my dad and watching sports with my dad.

🏸 MARK TEIXEIRA, PROFESSIONAL BASEBALL PLAYER 🏸

It is a known fact that
every man's heart is set
on having a daughter.

🏸 FRANÇOISE SAGAN, WRITER 🏸

I've been to war. I've raised twins.
If I had a choice, I'd rather go to war.

◖ GEORGE W. BUSH, 43RD PRESIDENT OF THE UNITED STATES ◗

I think that my strong determination for justice
comes from the very strong, dynamic personality of
my father . . . I have rarely ever met a person more
fearless and courageous than my father . . . The
thing that I admire most about my dad is his genuine
Christian character. He is a man of real integrity,
deeply committed to moral and ethical principles.
He is conscientious in all of his undertakings . . .
If I had a problem I could always call Daddy.

◖ MARTIN LUTHER KING JR., CIVIL RIGHTS ADVOCATE ◗

There's no pillow quite so soft
as a father's strong shoulder.

RICHARD L. EVANS, MEMBER OF THE QUORUM
OF THE TWELVE APOSTLES OF THE CHURCH OF
JESUS CHRIST OF LATTER-DAY SAINTS

I remember my daughter Deni coming along, and she was so pure and caring of everybody and everything. And somehow, this little being managed to get around all the obstacles—the gun turrets, the walls, the moats, the sentries—that were wrapped around my heart. My heart at that time needed her. . . . I think it's the best thing going, parenthood.

⋈ WOODY HARRELSON, ACTOR ⋈

A man never *stands* as tall as when he *kneels* to help a child.

KNIGHTS OF PYTHAGORAS

No music is so pleasant to my ears as that word—father.

LYDIA MARIA CHILD, WOMEN'S RIGHTS ACTIVIST

When you have kids, there's no such thing as quality time. There's just time. There's no, "Ooh, his graduation's better than going to the mall." It's all kind of equal. Changing her diaper and her winning a contest—it's all good.

CHRIS ROCK, COMEDIAN

Men should always change diapers. It's a very rewarding experience. It's mentally cleansing. It's like washing dishes, but imagine if the dishes were your kids, so you really love the dishes.

⟶ CHRIS MARTIN, MUSICIAN ⟵

Being Chinese immigrants in the United States, it was important for my parents to maintain ties that went back a long time. They led by example. My dad didn't bring his work pressures home. We were always aware of them and would go as kids to his office and run around. But when he came home, he was able to leave things behind, at least from our perspective, and focus on us.

C.C. PEI, SON OF I.M. PEI, ARCHITECT OF THE LOUVRE PYRAMID

There is no teacher equal to
mother and there's nothing more
contagious than the dignity of a father.

AMIT RAY, WRITER

I love my father as the stars—
he's a bright shining example
and a happy twinkling
in my heart.

TERRI GUILLEMETS, WRITER

Be a dad. Don't be "Mom's assistant." . . . Fathers have skills that they never use at home. You run a landscaping business and you can't dress and feed a four-year-old? Take it on. Spend time with your kids and have your own ideas about what they need. It won't take away your manhood; it will give it to you.

◖ LOUIS C.K., COMEDIAN ◗

A good father is one of the most unsung, unpraised, unnoticed, and yet one of the most valuable assets in our society.

◖ BILLY GRAHAM, CHRISTIAN EVANGELIST MINISTER ◗

I don't mind looking into the mirror and seeing my father.

◈ MICHAEL DOUGLAS, ACTOR ◈

My father used to say that it's never too late to do anything you wanted to do. And he said, "You never know what you can accomplish until you try."

◈ MICHAEL JORDAN, PROFESSIONAL BASKETBALL PLAYER ◈

One night a father overheard his son pray: "Dear God, make me the kind of man my Daddy *is*." Later that night, the father prayed: "Dear God, make me the kind of man my son *wants me to be*."

ANONYMOUS

Being a father has been, without a doubt, my greatest source of achievement, pride and inspiration. Fatherhood has taught me about unconditional love, reinforced the importance of giving back and taught me how to be a better person.

NAVEEN JAIN, ENTREPRENEUR

When a father gives to his son, both laugh;
when a son gives to his father, both cry.

▷ WILLIAM SHAKESPEARE, WRITER ◁

A father is the driving force
of the family who is always
content to take a back seat.

▷ LINDA POINDEXTER, WRITER ◁

Son, brother, father, lover, friend.
There is room in the heart for all
the affections, as there is room in
heaven for all the stars.

❧ VICTOR HUGO, WRITER ☙

The most important thing in the
world is family and love.

❧ JOHN WOODEN, BASKETBALL COACH ☙

I felt something impossible for me to explain in words. Then when they took her away, it hit me. I got scared all over again and began to feel giddy. Then it came to me—I was a father.

◁ NAT KING COLE, MUSICIAN ▷

I was raised in the greatest of homes . . . just a really great dad, and I miss him so much . . . he was a good man, a real simple man. . . . Very faithful, always loved my mom, always provided for the kids, and just a lot of fun.

◁ MAX LUCADO, WRITER ▷

A man finds out what is meant by a spitting image when he tries to feed cereal to his infant.

IMOGENE FAY, WRITER

One of the greatest gifts my father gave me—unintentionally—was witnessing the courage with which he bore adversity. We had a bit of a rollercoaster life with some really challenging financial periods. He was always unshaken, completely tranquil, the same ebullient, laughing, jovial man.

📣 BEN OKRI, WRITER 📣

One father can support twelve children, but twelve children cannot support one father.

📣 FRENCH PROVERB 📣

To me, having kids is the *ultimate* job in life. I want to be most successful at being a good father.

NICK LACHEY, MUSICIAN

My role model is my dad.

Being a great father is like shaving. No matter how good you shaved today, you have to do it again tomorrow.

**I imagine God to be like my father.
My father was always the voice of certainty
in my life. Certainty in the wisdom, certainty in
the path, certainty always in God. For me God
is certainty in everything. Certainty that
everything is good and everything is God.**

❧ YEHUDA BERG, WRITER ❧

I decided in my life that I would
do nothing that did not reflect
positively on my father's life.

❧ SIDNEY POITIER, ACTOR ❧

My dad is my hero.

❧ HARRY CONNICK JR., MUSICIAN ❧

I mean, I look at my dad. He was twenty
when he started having a family, and he was
always the coolest dad. He did everything for
his kids, and he never made us feel like he
was pressured. I know that it must be a
great feeling to be a guy like that.

❧ ADAM SANDLER, ACTOR ❧

The sooner you treat your son as a man,
the sooner he will be one.

JOHN DRYDEN, WRITER

My dad was my best friend and greatest role model. He was an amazing dad, coach, mentor, soldier, husband, and friend.

TIGER WOODS, PROFESSIONAL GOLFER

You don't have to deserve your mother's love. You have to deserve your father's. He's more particular.

❧ ROBERT FROST, WRITER ☙

If you know his father and grandfather you may trust his son.

❧ MOROCCAN PROVERB ☙

This is the price you pay for having a great father. You get the wonder, the joy, the tender moments—and you get the tears at the end, too.

❦ HARLAN COBEN, WRITER ❦

The best thing about being a dad?
Well, I think it's just the thing that every
man wants—to have a son and heir.

❦ GEORGE BEST, PROFESSIONAL SOCCER PLAYER ❦

One word of *command* from me is obeyed by millions . . . but I cannot get my three daughters . . . to come down to breakfast on time.

VISCOUNT ARCHIBALD WAVELL, SENIOR OFFICER OF THE BRITISH ARMY

I am not ashamed to say that no man
I ever met was my father's equal,
and I never loved any other man as much.

⊱ HEDY LAMARR, ACTRESS ⊰

There must always be a struggle between
a father and son, while one aims at power
and the other at independence.

⊱ SAMUEL JOHNSON, WRITER ⊰

It's only when you grow up and step back from him—or leave him for your own career and your own home—it's only then that you can measure [your father's] greatness and fully appreciate it.

MARGARET TRUMAN, SINGER AND WRITER

It is a wise father that knows his own child.

WILLIAM SHAKESPEARE, WRITER

Nearly every man is a firm believer in heredity until his son makes a fool of himself.

⧽ HERBERT V. PROCHNOW, BANKING EXECUTIVE ⧼

I want to congratulate all the men out there who are working diligently to be good fathers whether they are stepfathers, or biological fathers or just spiritual fathers.

⧽ T.D. JAKES, PASTOR AND WRITER ⧼

It is easier for a father to have children than for children to have a real father.

➤ POPE JOHN XXIII ◄

I would want my legacy to be that I was a great son, father and friend.

➤ DANTE HALL, PROFESSIONAL FOOTBALL PLAYER ◄

The debt of gratitude we owe our mother and father goes forward, not backward. What we owe our parents is the bill presented to us by our children.

NANCY FRIDAY, WRITER

My dad is my best friend, my father, and my boss. When I do something that is exciting and he likes it, it feels three times as good as you can imagine.

DAVID LAUREN, SON OF FASHION DESIGNER RALPH LAUREN

[O]ur children need our deep involvement in their lives. If this period [the early years] of primitive needs and primitive caretaking passes without us, it is lost forever. We can be involved in other ways, but never again on this profoundly intimate level.

🕊 AUGUSTUS Y. NAPIER, WRITER AND FAMILY THERAPIST 🕊

I can definitely say the older I've got the better I've become at being a dad and a husband.

🕊 ROD STEWART, MUSICIAN 🕊

You don't raise heroes, you raise sons. And if you treat them like *sons*, they'll turn out to be *heroes*, even if it's just in your own eyes.

WALTER SCHIRRA JR., PILOT

Fathers are what give daughters
away to other men who aren't nearly good
enough, so they can have grandchildren
who are smarter than anybody's.

▶ PAUL HARVEY, RADIO BROADCASTER ◀

**My dad is the backbone of our
family. Any problem that I've ever
had, he's always been there for me.**

▶ WHITNEY HOUSTON, MUSICIAN ◀

Lately all my friends are worried that they're turning into their fathers. I'm worried I'm not.

📣 DAN ZEVIN, WRITER 📣

Mothers play an important role as the heart of the home, but this in no way lessens the equally important role fathers should play, as head of the home, in nurturing, training, and loving their children.

📣 EZRA TAFT BENSON, 13TH PRESIDENT OF THE CHURCH OF JESUS CHRIST OF LATTER-DAY SAINTS 📣

Having a child ends forever a man's boyhood, if not his boyishness. Having a child means that the son has, in a real sense, become his father. Sons are for fathers the twice-told tale.

VICTORIA SECUNDA, WRITER

When it comes to Father's Day,
I will remember my dad for both being
there to nurture me and also for the times
he gave me on my own to cultivate my own
interests and to nurture my own spirit.

JENNIFER GRANT, ACTRESS

**Of all nature's gifts to the human race, what is
sweeter to a man than his children?**

CICERO, PHILOSOPHER AND POLITICIAN

I'm a father; that's what matters most. Nothing matters more.

GORDON BROWN, BRITISH POLITICIAN

But the world hinges on good fathers and those who would be the merchants of confidence.

MICHELLE FRANKLIN, WRITER

My first call is always to my dad. It's really rad. What had initially drove my dad and me apart—all my stunts and antics— has brought us together, closer than we've ever been. My dad's been a huge part of my team.

STEVE-O, TELEVISION PERSONALITY

We think our fathers fools,
so wise we grow;
Our wiser sons, no doubt,
will think us so.

ALEXANDER POPE, WRITER

I've said it before, but it's absolutely true:
My mother gave me my drive, but my father gave
me my dreams. Thanks to him, I could see a future.

LIZA MINNELLI, ACTRESS AND MUSICIAN

To this day I cannot see a bright daffodil, a proud gladiola, or a smooth eggplant without *thinking of Papa*. Like his plants and trees, I grew up as a part of his garden.

I pray to be a good servant to God, a father, a husband, a son, a friend, a brother, an uncle, a good neighbor, a good leader to those who look up to me, a good follower to those who are serving God and doing the right thing.

🕊 MARK WAHLBERG, ACTOR 🕊

**My Dad was my biggest supporter.
He never put pressure on me.**

BOBBY ORR, PROFESSIONAL HOCKEY PLAYER

One father is more than a
hundred schoolmasters.

GEORGE HERBERT, WRITER

You fathers will understand.
You have a little girl. She looks up to you.
You're her oracle. You're her hero.
And then the day comes when she gets
her first permanent wave and goes to
her first real party, and from that day on,
you're in a constant state of panic.

SPENCER TRACY, ACTOR,
AS STANLEY T. BANKS IN *FATHER OF THE BRIDE*

My dad encouraged me to quit my job and pursue the life that I am about to have. He got excited with me. He was the first one to tell me that I could do it. I am 30 years old, and I still find great power in my own dad telling me it's possible. I still find great power in my own dad telling me I can do it.

🕬 DAN PEARCE, WRITER 🕬

My father always used to say that when you die, if you've got five real friends, then you've had a great life.

🕬 LEE IACOCCA, BUSINESSMAN 🕬

I had no expectations
about fatherhood, really, but it's
definitely a journey I'm glad to be
taking. Number one, it's a great
learning experience. When my
mother told me it's a 24/7 job,
she wasn't kidding.

CHRISTOPHER MELONI, ACTOR

I love my dad. It's fair to say that I probably would not have thought of politics had I not seen my mom and dad involved in politics.

➤ MITT ROMNEY, POLITICIAN ◄

Safe, for a child, is his father's hand, holding him tight.

➤ MARION C. GARRETTY, WRITER ◄

I would say my greatest achievement in life right now—my greatest achievement period is—and I'm still trying to achieve it—is to be a wonderful father to my kids.

BO JACKSON, PROFESSIONAL FOOTBALL AND BASEBALL PLAYER

To show a child what has once delighted you, to find the child's delight added to your own, so that there is now a double delight seen in the glow of trust and affection, this is happiness.

J.B. PRIESTLEY, WRITER

What matters to me is not how I look, but the person inside, the one who grew up as—and is forever proud to be—the daughter of Bill Shepherd.

⋈ CYBILL SHEPHERD, ACTRESS ⋈

Old as she was, she still missed her daddy sometimes.

⋈ GLORIA NAYLOR, WRITER ⋈

A good father believes that he does wisely to encourage enterprise, productive skill, prudent self-denial, and judicious expenditure on the part of his son.

WILLIAM GRAHAM SUMNER, SOCIOLOGIST

Daddy's favorite tools are numbered among a child's favorite toys. Every kid wants to get her hands on Dad's retracting tape measure and his hammer. One father told me that his kids had taken over his under-car creeper as their favorite riding toy and he has trouble getting it back when he wants to change the oil.

ST. CLAIR ADAMS SULLIVAN, WRITER

Being a father helps me
be more responsible . . .
you see more things than
you've ever seen.

KID ROCK, MUSICIAN

Without my dad, I wouldn't be here.

MARIA SHARAPOVA, PROFESSIONAL TENNIS PLAYER

Children need love, especially
when they do not deserve it.

HAROLD S. HUBERT, WRITER

If a country is to be corruption free
and become a nation of beautiful minds,
I strongly feel there are three key societal
members who can make a difference. They
are the father, the mother, and the teacher.

A.P.J. ABDUL KALAM, 11TH PRESIDENT OF INDIA

Fathers seem powerful and overwhelming to their daughters. Let her see your soft side. Express your feelings and reactions. Tell her where you came from and how you got there. Let her see that you have fears, failures, anxious times, hurts, just like hers, even though you may look flawless to her.

STELLA CHESS, PSYCHIATRIST AND WRITER

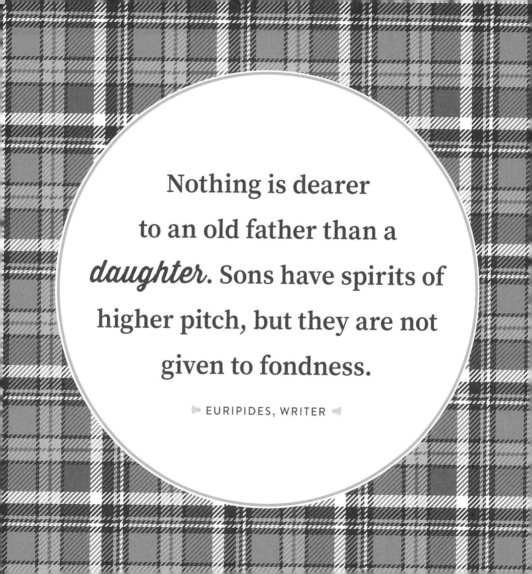

Nothing is dearer
to an old father than a
daughter. Sons have spirits of
higher pitch, but they are not
given to fondness.

EURIPIDES, WRITER

A father is a man who expects his son to be
as good a man as he meant to be.

▷ FRANK A. CLARK, WRITER ◁

It was my father who
taught us that an immigrant
must work twice as hard
as anybody else, that he
must never give up.

▷ ZINEDINE ZIDANE, PROFESSIONAL SOCCER PLAYER ◁

The first handshake in life is the greatest of all: the clasp of an infant's fist around a parent's finger.

MARK BELTAIRE, JOURNALIST

I feel more and more like "myself" these days. Before becoming a father, I can remember a low-level feeling of somehow not quite being myself.

B.D. WONG, ACTOR

Each father wants their sons
to be just like them, really.

⊳ ZIGGY MARLEY, MUSICIAN ⊲

A child enters your home and for the next twenty years makes so much noise you can hardly stand it. The child departs, leaving the house so silent you think you are going mad.

⊳ JOHN ANDREW HOLMES, WRITER ⊲

Dad, you couldn't have done it better. You're actually pretty amazing especially because I'm fully aware of the demanding brat I was.

◁ JOHN TRAVOLTA, ACTOR ▷

I grew up around lots of men—my father, my brothers, my uncles—so I wasn't intimidated by them.

◁ DOLLY PARTON, MUSICIAN ▷

I'm quite sensitive to women. I saw how my sister got treated by boyfriends. I read this thing that said when you are *in a relationship* with a woman, imagine how you would feel if you were her father. That's been my approach, for the most part.

ORLANDO BLOOM, ACTOR

The relationship of a parent with a teenager is shot through with ambiguities and hypocrisies, large and small—the child's dependence and resentment, the parent's self-indulgence and prohibitions. But somewhere within this uneasy mix, in the best of families . . . both parent and child know which lines should not be crossed; the child's sense of privacy, the parent's sense of propriety. A delicate balance preserved until, as adults, both sides can either laugh about it or forget it.

☙ RICHARD NORTH PATTERSON, WRITER ❧

Allow children to be happy in their own way, for what better way will they ever find?

◈ SAMUEL JOHNSON, WRITER ◈

I had heard all those things about fatherhood, how great it is. But it's greater than I'd ever expected—I had no idea Quinton would steal my heart the way he has. From the minute I laid eyes on him, I knew nobody could ever wrestle him away from me.

◈ BURT REYNOLDS, ACTOR ◈

I think my dad is a lot cooler than other dads. He still acts like he's still seventeen.

MILEY CYRUS, MUSICIAN

I love my father so much and he has taught me so many things.

BEYONCÉ KNOWLES-CARTER, MUSICIAN

There is no greater name for a leader than mother or father. There is no leadership more important than parenthood.

SHERI L. DEW, WRITER

Don't demand respect, as a parent. Demand civility and insist on honesty. But respect is something you must earn— with kids as well as with adults.

WILLIAM ATTWOOD, LAWYER AND WRITER

For me, the most important thing that I have to accomplish is to be a good father. That's the most difficult challenge of my life. That's the most important thing for me, more than films.

ALEJANDRO GONZÁLEZ IÑÁRRITU, DIRECTOR

My father taught me you have to believe in yourself and run on your own track.

JENNIFER GREY, ACTRESS

How easily a father's tenderness recalled, and how quickly a son's offenses vanish, at the slightest word of repentance!

MOLIÈRE, WRITER AND ACTOR

More broadly across time and cultures, it seems, one perennial piece of advice to fathers has been the importance of acting tenderly toward their children.

DAVID BLANKENHORN, FOUNDER AND PRESIDENT OF THE INSTITUTE FOR AMERICAN VALUES

As a father, physician and nurse, I have a special place in my heart for children, and I know the brief window of opportunity we have to teach them simple lessons that can lead to a lifetime of good health.

RICHARD CARMONA, PHYSICIAN, POLICE OFFICER, AND POLITICIAN

Raising children is part joy and
part guerrilla warfare.

◖ ED ASNER, ACTOR ◗

At times I've got a really big ego. But I'll tell
you the best thing about me. I'm some guy's dad; I'm
some little gal's dad. When I die, if they say I
was Annie's husband and Zachary John and Anna
Kate's father, boy, that's enough for me to be
remembered by. That's more than enough.

◖ JOHN DENVER, MUSICIAN ◗

As my father used to tell me, the only *true sign* of success in life is being able to do for a living that which makes you happy.

AL YANKOVIC, MUSICIAN

I learned from the example of my father that the manner in which one endures what must be endured is more important than the thing that must be endured.

DEAN ACHESON, STATESMAN AND LAWYER

The best brought-up children are those who have seen their parents as they are. Hypocrisy is not the parents' first duty.

GEORGE BERNARD SHAW, WRITER

Fathers are blind to the faults of their daughters.

⊱ ANONYMOUS ⊰

So my father was a person who never lied to me. If I had a question, he answered it. I knew a lot of things at a young age because I was intrigued.

⊱ NICK CANNON, MUSICIAN ⊰

Parents ought, through their own behavior and the values by which they live, to provide direction for their children. But they need to rid themselves of the idea that there are surefire methods which, when well applied, will produce certain predictable results. Whatever we do with and for our children ought to flow from our understanding of and our feelings for the particular situation and the relation we wish to exist between us and our child.

BRUNO BETTELHEIM, PSYCHOLOGIST

Whoever does not have a good father should procure one.

When you have children yourself, you begin to understand what you owe your parents.

My father was a *man of love*. He always loved me to death. He worked hard in the fields, but my father never hit me. Never. I don't ever remember a really cross, unkind word from my father.

JOHNNY CASH, MUSICIAN

A baby has a way of making a man out of his father and a boy out of his grandfather.

☙ ANGIE PAPADAKIS, WRITER ❧

I cannot think of any need in childhood as strong as the need for a father's protection.

☙ SIGMUND FREUD, AUSTRIAN PSYCHOANALYST ❧

If you can give your son only one gift,
let it be enthusiasm.

BRUCE BARTON, WRITER AND POLITICIAN

**I look at my father. He is one of my heroes.
He is such an incredible, classy man. He was such
a great father and such a great husband in so many
ways, and we lived through some pretty tough times
losing my mom. When I see all that he did, I think,
"Wow, that's a really wonderful man."**

EMMANUELLE CHRIQUI, ACTRESS

My dad had been shortstop when he was in college, and you know, when you're a kid, you want to be just like your dad.

❧ DEREK JETER, PROFESSIONAL BASEBALL PLAYER ☙

Children aren't happy with nothing to ignore, and that is what parents were created for.

❧ OGDEN NASH, WRITER ☙

To be a successful father . . . there's one absolute rule: when you have a kid, don't look at it for the first two years.

ERNEST HEMINGWAY, WRITER

There have been many times when I thought other people might be better singers or better musicians or prettier than me, but then I would hear Daddy's voice telling me to never say never, and I would find a way to squeeze an extra inch or two out of what God had given me.

BARBARA MANDRELL, MUSICIAN

When I was 5, my father was very much my hero. And he ran for political office in a very thankless campaign for a very thankless position. And he did it because his mother had instilled in him, if you are someone who has the capacity to make a great change, you have the responsibility.

HOWARD WARREN BUFFETT, PHILANTHROPIST AND BUSINESSMAN

How pleasant it is for a father to sit at his child's board. It is like an aged man reclining under the shadow of an oak which he has planted.

SIR WALTER SCOTT, WRITER

My dad's music was a great inspiration to me.

JULIAN LENNON, MUSICIAN

I always joke that my kids' favorite holiday is Father's Day. They love the way I celebrate the occasion by writing each of them a thank-you letter and a generous check. It's my way of letting them know how much I appreciate the great pleasure and privilege of being their dad.

WAYNE DYER, WRITER

I just owe everything to my father [and] it's passionately interesting for me that the things that I learned in a small town, in a very modest home, are just the things that I believe have won the election.

MARGARET THATCHER, FIRST FEMALE PRIME MINISTER OF THE UNITED KINGDOM

What a father says to his children is not heard by the world, but it will be heard by posterity.

JEAN PAUL RICHTER, WRITER

It isn't that
I'm a weak father,
it's just that she's a
strong daughter.

HENRY FONDA, ACTOR

Many people now believe that if fathers are more interested in raising children than they were, children and sons in particular will learn that men can be warm and supportive of others as well as be high achievers. Thus, fathers' involvement may be beneficial not because it will help support traditional male roles, but because it will help to break them down.

⊯ JOSEPH PLECK, WRITER ⊰

Now that I'm a parent, I understand why my father was in a bad mood a lot.

⊯ ADAM SANDLER, ACTOR ⊰

My father considered a walk
among the mountains as the
equivalent of churchgoing.

⊰ ALDOUS HUXLEY, WRITER ⊱

If I chance to talk a little wild,
forgive me;
I had it from my father.

⊰ WILLIAM SHAKESPEARE, WRITER ⊱

My father said there were
two kinds of people in the world:
givers and takers. The takers may eat
better, but the givers sleep better.

◖ MARLO THOMAS, ACTRESS ◗

**We live in the past to an astonishing
degree, the myth we live by, the presumptions
we make. Nobody can look in the mirror
and not see his mother or father.**

◖ E.L. DOCTOROW, WRITER ◗

I try to live my life like my father lives his. He always takes care of everyone else first. He won't even start eating until he's sure everyone else in the family has started eating. Another thing: My dad never judges me by whether I win or lose.

BEN ROETHLISBERGER, PROFESSIONAL FOOTBALL PLAYER

Fathers are ironic,
they want *democracy*
in their country
but dictatorship in
their home.

AMIT KALANTRI, WRITER

My prescription for success is based on something my father always used to tell me: You should never try to be better than someone else, but you should never cease trying to be the best that you can be.

⊳ JOHN WOODEN, BASKETBALL COACH ⊲

He adopted a role called Being a Father so that his child would have something mythical and infinitely important: a Protector.

⊳ TOM WOLFE, WRITER ⊲

[Becoming a father] changes your views on most everything you look at in life, and the great thing about it is no matter what kind of day I have, she's always there waiting for me when I get home.

ROBERTO LUONGO, PROFESSIONAL HOCKEY PLAYER

There are only two lasting bequests we can hope to give our children. One of these is roots; the other, wings.

Words have an awesome impact. The impression made by a father's voice can set in motion an entire trend of life.

I am so proud of my father; he is the
biggest example of success and courage
I have ever seen in my life. He is the emperor
of my kingdom. Of course, my father IS an emperor,
his name is Asoka, the greatest emperor ruled in
India. Moreover, as the name says, he is "without
sorrow" and the slayer of our sorrows.

AMA H. VANNIARACHCHY, WRITER

Children have never been
very good at listening to their elders,
but they have never failed to imitate them.

JAMES BALDWIN, WRITER

A couple of years before he died, I kissed my father goodbye. He said, "Son, you haven't kissed me since you were a little boy." It went straight to my heart, and I kissed him whenever I saw him after that, and my sons and I always kiss whenever we meet.

TERRY WOGAN, IRISH RADIO BROADCASTER

My dad was the biggest influence on my life because he was never boring.

CHRISTIAN BALE, ACTOR

No man can possibly know what life means, what the world means, what anything means, until he has a child and loves it. And then the whole universe changes and nothing will ever seem exactly as it seemed before.

LAFCADIO HEARN, WRITER

You are your daughter's hero.

ELAINE S. DALTON, 13TH PRESIDENT OF THE
YOUNG WOMEN ORGANIZATION OF THE CHURCH OF
JESUS CHRIST OF LATTER-DAY SAINTS

My father didn't tell me how to live; he lived, and let me watch him do it.

CLARENCE BUDINGTON KELLAND, WRITER

He always said, "Babe, pay your own way. Don't owe anybody anything." And that's the way I've lived.

LILY TOMLIN, ACTRESS

He loves his children not because everything in them is lovely and according to his liking, but because there is a real incomprehensible bond which is stronger than fiction.

▷ LEROY BROWNLOW, WRITER ◁

A *truly rich man* is one whose children run into his arms when his hands are empty.

The best word to describe my father? Thoughtful. There was a tender quality to Dad that his sense of fun could sometimes mask. But, above all, he was sensitive and looked out for those he loved.

JENNIFER GRANT, ACTRESS

My father made me who I am. He gave me a basketball and told me to play with the ball, sleep with the ball, dream with the ball. Just don't take it to school. I used it as a pillow, and it never gave me a stiff neck.

SHAQUILLE O'NEAL, PROFESSIONAL BASKETBALL PLAYER

What children expect from grownups is not to be "understood," but only to be loved, even though this love may be expressed clumsily or in sternness. Intimacy does not exist between generations—only trust.

⟿ CARL ZUCKER, WRITER ⟿

My father was strict and always taught me, no matter who it is, everybody is an uncle. To me, everybody was someone I respect like family. I grew up with that.

MARIANO RIVERA, PROFESSIONAL BASEBALL PLAYER

When you, too, are a father, and you hear
your children's little voices . . . You will feel that
those little ones are akin to every drop in your veins,
that they are the very flower of your life . . . you
will cleave so closely to them that you seem to feel
every movement that they make.

🕮 HONORÉ DE BALZAC, WRITER 🕮

Being a father can "unreason" your
worldview, or at least make it very flexible,
and that can create all sorts of fun and insights.
It's sad that children's open-eyed wonder and sense
of play begin to fade as they approach adolescence.
One grand function of fathering is to keep
the fading to a minimum.

CLYDE EDGERTON, WRITER

Give a little love to a child, and you
get a great deal back.

JOHN RUSKIN, ART CRITIC

It is much easier to *become* a father than to *be* one.

KENT NERBURN, WRITER

Dads don't need to be tall
and broad-shouldered and clever.
Love makes them so.

PAM BROWN, WRITER

What my father especially taught me was to
not always take the safe road, the easy road.
If you are going to do good work,
you have to risk failing badly.

NATASHA RICHARDSON, ACTRESS

To her the name of father was another name for love.

⏵ FANNY FERN, NEWSPAPER COLUMNIST ⏴

It is my pleasure that my children are free and happy and unrestrained by parental tyranny. Love is the chain whereby to bind a child to its parents.

⏵ ABRAHAM LINCOLN, 16TH PRESIDENT OF THE UNITED STATES ⏴

A man's fatherliness
is enriched as much by his
acceptance of his feminine and
childlike strivings as it is by his
memories of tender closeness with
his own father. A man who has
been able to accept tenderness from
his father is able later in life to be
tender with his own children.

LOUISE J. KAPLAN, PSYCHOANALYST AND WRITER

Becoming a father increases your capacity for love and your level of patience. It opens up another door in a person—a door which you may not even have known was there. That's what I feel with my son. There's suddenly another level of love that expands. My son is my greatest joy, out of everything in my life.

KYLE MACLACHLAN, ACTOR

It's a wonderful feeling when your father becomes not a god but a man to you—when he comes down from the mountain and you see he's this man with weaknesses. And you love him as this whole being, not as a figurehead.

Being a father makes
everything in the world
make sense.

**Fatherhood is a very natural thing;
it's not something that shakes up my
life but rather it enriches it.**

My father served 26 years
in the Air Force as a pilot and a pioneer
in our missile programs. I learned early
about the *sacrifices* a family makes
when a member is repeatedly deployed,
and also the fulfillment that comes from
serving our country. My brother, my son
and I all became Marines.

JIM WEBB, U.S. POLITICIAN AND WRITER

Govern a small family as you would cook a small fish—very gently.

CHINESE PROVERB

All the feeling which my father could not put into words was in his hand—any dog, child, or horse would recognize the kindness of it.

FREYA STARK, WRITER

My father always said, "I don't care if you're a ditch digger, as long as you're the best ditch digger in the world."

TWYLA THARP, DANCER

It is better to bind your children to you by a feeling of respect, and by gentleness, than by fear.

TERENCE, WRITER

We never know the love of a parent until we become parents ourselves.

🖾 HENRY WARD BEECHER,
CONGREGATIONALIST CLERGYMAN AND SPEAKER 🖾

Happiness does not come from football awards. It's terrible to correlate happiness with football. Happiness comes from a good job, being able to feed your wife and kids. I don't dream football, I dream the American dream—two cars in a garage, be a happy father.

BARRY SANDERS, PROFESSIONAL FOOTBALL PLAYER

Every father knows at once too much and too little about his own son.

❧ FANNY FERN, NEWSPAPER COLUMNIST ❧

I have never been a material girl. My father always told me never to love anything that cannot love you back.

❧ IMELDA MARCOS, 10TH FIRST LADY OF THE PHILIPPINES ❧

My father used to play with my brother and me in the yard. Mother would come out and say, "You're tearing up the grass!" "We're not raising grass," Dad would reply. "We're raising boys."

HARMON KILLEBREW, PROFESSIONAL BASEBALL PLAYER

My father never was
and isn't a mean man. You know,
he never was ruthless. And he
succeeded in life without sticking it to
anybody. And that's a *great example*
for a man, a strong man, a man's
man, to give to his children. You can
succeed, you can be successful, without
walking over somebody.

MARIA SHRIVER, JOURNALIST

An atmosphere of trust, love, and humor can nourish extraordinary human capacity. One key is authenticity: parents acting as people, not as roles.

MARILYN FERGUSON, WRITER

The meaningful role of the father of the bride was played out long before the church music began. It stretched across those years of infancy and puberty, adolescence and young adulthood. That's when she needs you at her side.

I don't care what they say about me when I'm through with sports. I don't want to be known as anything else in life but a great father.

My father always said, "Do your best and piss on the rest." And I think there's a lot of truth to that, because if you've done your best, there's not a hell of a lot more you can do about something.

KADEE STRICKLAND, ACTRESS

My father was the funniest guy I ever met. I'm not sure if I stole his stuff or if I inherited it.

CHEVY CHASE, COMEDIAN

Your son and your daughter need an excellent father more than an excellent college.

NICK VUJICIC, MOTIVATIONAL SPEAKER

My father taught me not to overthink things, that nothing will ever be perfect, so just keep moving and do your best.

SCOTT EASTWOOD, ACTOR

My father always taught by telling stories about his experiences. His lessons were about morality and art and what insects and birds and human beings had in common. He told me what it meant to be a man and to be a Black man. He taught me about love and responsibility, about beauty, and how to make gumbo.

WALTER MOSLEY, WRITER

It is impossible to please all the world and one's father.

☙ JEAN DE LA FONTAINE, WRITER ❧

Most American children suffer too much mother and too little father.

☙ GLORIA STEINEM, JOURNALIST AND SOCIAL ACTIVIST ❧

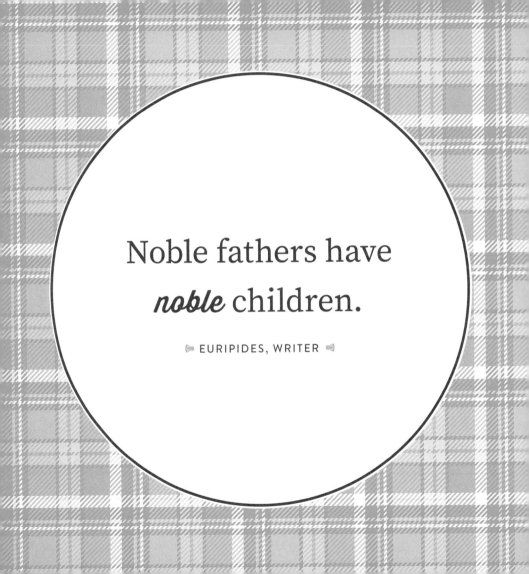

Noble fathers have *noble* children.

EURIPIDES, WRITER

I tell people I'm a stand-up comedian
two hours a week. The rest of the time,
I'm somebody's husband, I'm somebody's father.
I'm a man. I take great pride in that.

STEVE HARVEY, COMEDIAN

Children want to feel instinctively
that their father is behind them as solid
as a mountain, but, like a mountain,
is something to look up to.

DOROTHY THOMPSON, JOURNALIST

Your children need your presence
more than your presents.

➤ JESSE JACKSON, CIVIL RIGHTS ACTIVIST,
BAPTIST MINISTER, AND POLITICIAN ◄

You've got to do your
own growing, no matter how
tall your grandfather was.

➤ IRISH PROVERB ◄

More by example than by word, my father taught me logical reasoning, compassion, love of others, honesty, and discipline applied with understanding.

PAUL D. BOYER, BIOCHEMIST

My father was a Tuskegee Airmen captain in the Air Force and a very strong personality. He believed in fairness and ethics and living up to the commitments you make to others. He ultimately became a judge, and he would talk to me over and over about how important it is to be fair.

By profession I am a soldier and take pride in that fact. But I am prouder—infinitely prouder—to be a father.

DOUGLAS MACARTHUR, U.S. ARMY GENERAL

My father used to say, "Let them see you and not the suit. That should be secondary."

CARY GRANT, ACTOR

A man prides himself on his strength—
but when his child is born he discovers
that strength is not enough, and
that he must learn gentleness.

❧ PAM BROWN, WRITER ☙

**I'm a first-time father, and it was amazing
to me to learn that my son could actually use
sign language before the spoken word. I could see
this intelligence in his eyes before he could speak:
how he could understand what was going on
around him and was frustrated by that.**

❧ MATT REEVES, WRITER AND DIRECTOR ☙

It's a *humbling* thing, having kids. One of my sons came to rehearsals, and now he says Daddy's job is "go play loud music."

TRENT REZNOR, MUSICIAN

Like many fathers,
he had a favorite ritual:
to put his whole family in
the car and drive somewhere.
It didn't matter where—what
mattered was that he was
behind the wheel.

SIGNE HAMMER, WRITER

I've always traveled with a picture of my daughter from 1989, her kindergarten school picture, that has "I love you, Daddy" written on it. She's always made fun of me because I never changed that picture out. It's like my resistance to her getting older. It was the first thing she'd ever written to me and it means the world to me.

⫘ KIEFER SUTHERLAND, ACTOR ⫘

The good-enough father is not simply
a knight in shining armor galloping to the occasional
rescue; he is there through good times and bad,
insisting on and delighting in his paternity every
pleasurable and painful step of the way.

⬧ VICTORIA SECUNDA, WRITER ⬧

The good part of having six kids is,
there's always one who wants to hug
you and say, "Daddy, I love you."

⬧ JOHN MCENROE, PROFESSIONAL TENNIS PLAYER ⬧

The kind of man who thinks that helping with the dishes is beneath him will also think that helping with the baby is beneath him, and then he certainly is not going to be a very successful father.

ELEANOR ROOSEVELT, U.S. POLITICIAN, DIPLOMAT, AND ACTIVIST

A father's calling is eternal and its importance transcends time.

⚑ EZRA TAFT BENSON, 13TH PRESIDENT OF THE CHURCH OF JESUS CHRIST OF LATTER-DAY SAINTS ⚑

Loving my son, building my son, touching my son, playing with my son, being with my son . . . these aren't tasks that only super dads can perform. These are tasks that every dad should perform. Always. Without fail.

🏶 DAN PEARCE, WRITER 🏶

The quality of a father can be seen in the goals, dreams and aspirations he sets not only for himself, but for his family.

🏶 REED MARKHAM, WRITER AND EDUCATOR 🏶

In the early years, I found a voice that was my voice and also partly *my father's voice*. But isn't that what you always do? Why do kids at 5 years old go into the closet and put their daddy's shoes on? Hey, my kids do it.

BRUCE SPRINGSTEEN, MUSICIAN

You've got to stand up and do your own battles. My daddy taught me that a long time ago, that you fight your own battles. The only way to shut everybody up is to win.

TERRY BRADSHAW, PROFESSIONAL FOOTBALL PLAYER

I loved those years of being Mr. Mom. One of the saddest days in my life was when Jennifer said, "Dad, I can wash my own hair."

BILLY CRYSTAL, COMEDIAN

Every day, my daddy
told me the same thing.
"Once a task is just begun,
never leave it till it's done.
Be the labour great or small,
do it well or not at all."

QUINCY JONES, RECORD PRODUCER AND COMPOSER

**A father is only capable of giving
what he has, and what he knows. A good
father gives all of himself that is good.**

VINCENT CARRELLA, GAME DEVELOPER AND WRITER

Parents teach in the toughest
school in the world—The School for
Making People. You are the board
of education, the principal, the
classroom teacher, and the janitor.

VIRGINIA SATIR, SOCIAL WORKER AND WRITER

Women's childhood relationships with their fathers are important to them all their lives.

▷ STELLA CHESS, CHILD PSYCHIATRIST ◁

I don't think you automatically become an enlightened person because you are a daddy. But they will change you, of course—their understanding of you puts you in a different place.

▷ JOHN HURT, ACTOR ◁

There are three stages of a man's life:
He believes in Santa Claus,
he doesn't believe in Santa Claus,
he is Santa Claus.

❧ ANONYMOUS ❧

Dads are stone skimmers, mud wallowers, water wallopers, ceiling swoopers, shoulder gallopers, upsy-downsy, over-and-through, round-and-about whooshers. Dads are smugglers and secret sharers.

[Fatherhood is] a time when you start to think about all the things your dad did when he was raising you. Why he did certain things and told you certain things. You *start to remember* things about your own dad.

DANIEL SEDIN, PROFESSIONAL HOCKEY PLAYER

[Fatherhood] is the most insanely amazing, most beautiful, unbelievable thing that can ever happen to you.

JUSTIN TIMBERLAKE, MUSICIAN

Anyone who tells you fatherhood is the greatest thing that can happen to you, they are understating it.

MIKE MYERS, ACTOR

My father gave me the greatest gift anyone could give another person: he believed in me.

≈ JIM VALVANO, BASKETBALL COACH ≈

It's like you have a child and you think, "Everything that I've done up until this point is insignificant in comparison to being a father." It's a beautiful, beautiful thing.

≈ VIN DIESEL, ACTOR ≈

When my father didn't have my hand,
he had my back.

🎀 LINDA POINDEXTER, WRITER 🎀

**When you become a parent,
you look at your parents differently.
You look at being a child differently.
It's an awakening, a revelation
that you have.**

🎀 PHILIP SEYMOUR HOFFMAN, ACTOR 🎀

My life has always been with my dad. Since I can remember, I was raised by my father my entire life. So he's kind of been that mom and father figure— always.

🎺 APOLO OHNO, PROFESSIONAL SPEEDSKATER 🎺

I'm sure there were times when I wish I had thought, "Gosh, that might really embarrass mom and dad," but our parents didn't raise us to think about them. They're very selfless and they wanted us to have as normal of a college life as possible. So really, we didn't think of any repercussions.

🔊 JENNA BUSH, JOURNALIST AND DAUGHTER OF GEORGE W. BUSH 🔊

My father was the guy on the block who said hi to everyone.

DAMON WAYANS, COMEDIAN

Every day of my life has been a gift from him. His lap had been my refuge from lightning and thunder. His arms had sheltered me from teenage heartbreak. His wisdom and understanding had sustained me as an adult.

NELLIE PIKE RANDALL, WRITER

My dad raised me with some good advice: "Always *tell the truth*. Always shoot from the hip. You might not have many friends, but you'll never have enemies, because people will always know where you're coming from."

🏴 PINK, MUSICIAN 🏴

My dear father! When I remember him, it is always with his arms open wide to love and comfort me.

▷ ISOBEL FIELD, STEPDAUGHTER OF ROBERT LOUIS STEVENSON ◁

My father . . . lived as if he were poured from iron, and loved his family with a vulnerability that was touching.

▷ MARI E. EVANS, WRITER ◁

My father was two men, one sympathetic and intuitional, the other critical and logical; altogether they formed a combination that could not be thrown off its feet.

JULIAN HAWTHORNE, WRITER

Me and my dad are friends. We're cool. I'll never be disappointed again, because I don't expect anything anymore from him. I just let him exist, and that's how we get along.

DRAKE, MUSICIAN

I remember being upset once and telling my dad I wasn't following through right, and he replied, "Nancy, it doesn't make any difference to a ball what you do after you hit it."

◈ NANCY LOPEZ, PROFESSIONAL GOLFER ◈

My dad's probably one of the kindest people in the world. When I was younger that's not how I was—I was a little spoiled brat.

LEONARDO DICAPRIO, ACTOR

Dad needs to show an incredible amount of respect and humor and friendship toward his mate so the kids understand their parents are sexy, they're fun, they do things together, they're best friends. Kids learn by example. If I respect Mom, they're going to respect Mom.

TIM ALLEN, COMEDIAN

My fondest and earliest memory of my father is being able to get in his lap and sit. I still to this day sit in his lap, and he loves it. I don't think you're ever too old for that.

🕊 HOLLY HESTON, DAUGHTER OF CHARLTON HESTON 🕊

The most important influence in my childhood was my father.

🕊 JACKSON DEFOREST KELLEY, ACTOR 🕊

He opened the jar of pickles
when no one else could. He was the
only one in the house who wasn't afraid
to go into the basement by himself. He
cut himself shaving, but no one kissed it
or got excited about it. It was understood
that when it rained, he got the car and
brought it around to the door. When
anyone was sick, he went out to get
the prescription filled. He took lots of
pictures . . . but he was never in them.

I never saw my dad cry. My son saw me cry. My dad never told me he loved me, and consequently I told Scott I loved him every other minute. The point is, I'll *make less mistakes* than my dad, my sons hopefully will make less mistakes than me, and their sons will make less mistakes than their dads.

JAMES CAAN, ACTOR

I think there's nothing better than laughing in life, so that's nice, to be thought of as someone who can make someone laugh. It's 'cause I think life is hard. You know, my dad was a really silly man. A great Irish silly man. And that's fine.

It wasn't like I was self-motivated.
My dad started me.
It was his dream before it was mine.

▷ VENUS WILLIAMS, PROFESSIONAL TENNIS PLAYER ◁

The history, the root, the strength of my father is the strength we now rest on.

▷ CAROLYN M. RODGERS, WRITER ◁

I modeled myself on my father. And this much at least was worthy of admiration: nothing downed his spirits for long.

☞ ELAINE FEINSTEIN, WRITER ☜

According to my parents, I just started drumming when I was two. I traveled with them from five to seven on the road, playing percussion. Between eight and twelve, my dad sort of prepared me by teaching me every aspect of road life.

☞ QUESTLOVE, MUSICIAN ☜

I was not close to my father, but he was very special to me. Whenever I did something as a little girl—learn to swim or act in a school play, for instance—he was fabulous. There would be this certain look in his eyes. It made me feel great.

⟫ DIANE KEATON, ACTRESS ⟪

Of course there were areas of safety; nothing could get at me if I curled up on my father's lap, holding his ear with one thumb tucked into it. . . . All about him was safe.

🪶 NAOMI MITCHISON, WRITER 🪶

One night at about two o'clock in the morning my father caught a man stealing bananas from our backyard. He went over to the man with his machete, took the bananas, cut the branch in half and said, "Here, you can have it." And then he said, "From now on, if you need anything from the back of our house, come to the front."

☙ CHI CHI RODRIGUEZ, PROFESSIONAL GOLFER ☙

I have never been jealous. Not even when my dad finished fifth grade a year before I did.

☙ JEFF FOXWORTHY, COMEDIAN ☙

There must've been hundreds of people cheering at some of those track meets, but *my father's voice* always found me. A simple "That's it, kid" and my feet grew wings.

⊲ MADISON RILEY, ACTRESS ⊳

My dad taught me from my youngest childhood memories through these connections with Aboriginal and tribal people that you must always protect people's sacred status, regardless of the past.

◄ STEVE IRWIN, NATURE EXPERT AND TELEVISION PERSONALITY ►

From my dad I learned to be good to people, to always be honest and straightforward. I learned hard work and perseverance.

◄ LUKE BRYAN, MUSICIAN ►

I've always had a burning desire to help people and make a difference in the world. I didn't know how I could do that in modelling when it can be such a fake world. But my dad told me I could make a difference by being true to myself and teaching people what I've learnt about spirituality, health and nutrition.

≈ MIRANDA KERR, MODEL ≈

Whenever I try to recall that long-ago first day at school, only one memory shines through: my father held my hand.

≈ MARCELENE COX, WRITER ≈

My dad used to say, "Just be yourself and you'll be fine," but it's really, really true.

◄ BELLAMY YOUNG, ACTRESS ►

My father, he was like the rock, the guy you went to with every problem.

◄ GWYNETH PALTROW, ACTRESS ►

My parents were kind of overprotective people. Me and my sister had to play in the backyard all the time. They bought us bikes for Christmas but wouldn't let us ride in the street, we had to ride in the backyard. Another Christmas, my dad got me a basketball hoop and put it in the middle of the lawn! You can't dribble on grass.

JIMMY FALLON, COMEDIAN

He was strong rather than profound. . . . I often wonder about him. In my struggle to be a writer, it was he who supported and backed me and explained me . . .

JOHN STEINBECK, WRITER

My dad said to me, "Work hard and be patient." It was the best advice he ever gave me. You have to put the hours in.

SIMON COWELL, TELEVISION PERSONALITY

**My dad was relaxed and casual and believed
in living in the present and having a good time.
He had a full life and enjoyed himself no
matter what happened.**

⊳ BING CROSBY, MUSICIAN ⊲

I know fame and power are
for the birds. But then life suddenly
comes into focus for me. And, ah, there
stand my kids. I love them.

⊳ LEE IACOCCA, BUSINESSMAN ⊲

My dad always said, "Champ, the measure of a man is not how *often* he is knocked down, but how *quickly* he gets up."

JOE BIDEN, 47TH VICE PRESIDENT OF THE UNITED STATES

A lot of people don't realize this, but probably the one person that gets made fun of in *South Park* more than anybody is my dad. Stan's father, Randy— my dad's name is Randy—that's my drawing of my dad; that's me doing my dad's voice. That is just my dad. Even Stan's last name, Marsh, was my dad's stepfather's name.

◈ TREY PARKER, ANIMATOR AND WRITER ◈

If my father had hugged me even once, I'd be an accountant right now.

☞ RAY ROMANO, COMEDIAN ☜

The most important thing about our time together was this: whatever his politics or view of the role of women, he never made me think there was anything I couldn't do.

☞ SUSAN KENNEY, WRITER ☜

My parents couldn't give me a whole lot of financial support, but they gave me good genes. My dad is a handsome son-of-a-gun, and my mom is beautiful. And I've definitely been the lucky recipient. So, thank you, Mom and Dad.

ASHTON KUTCHER, ACTOR

In my younger and more vulnerable years
my father gave me some advice that I've been
turning over in my mind ever since. "Whenever
you feel like criticizing any one," he told me,
"just remember that all the people in this world
haven't had the advantages that you've had."

⊳ F. SCOTT FITZGERALD, WRITER ⊲

I've had some amazing people in my life. Look at my
father—he came from a small fishing village of five
hundred people and at six foot four with giant ears
and a kind of very odd expression, thought he could
be a movie star. So go figure, you know?

⊳ KIEFER SUTHERLAND, ACTOR ⊲

The daily arguments over putting away the toys or practicing the piano defeat us so easily. We see them coming yet they frustrate us time and time again. In many cases, we are mothers and fathers who have managed budgets and unruly bosses and done difficult jobs well through sheer tenacity and dogged preparation. So why are we unable to persuade someone three feet tall to step into six inches of water at bathtime?

✇ CATHY RINDNER TEMPELSMAN, WRITER ✇

My dad has been a big influence on me, because he's always had his own business. He really taught me business sense and how to be a focused individual, but also how to have fun and make everyone around you have fun.

WIZ KHALIFA, MUSICIAN

SOURCES

http://dadgab.com/top-10-celebrity-dad-quotes/

http://parade.com/303081/viannguyen/fathers-day-2014-50-funny-and-inspiring-quotes-about-dads/3/

http://rollingout.com/2016/06/16/10-celebrity-dad-quotes-that-will-make-your-ovaries-burst/11/

http://thestir.cafemom.com/celebrities/121912/15_quotes_for_fathers_day

www.askmen.com/entertainment/galleries/best-quotes-on-fatherhood.html

www.bartleby.com/quotations/

www.brainyquote.com/quotes/topics/topic_fathersday3.html

www.brainyquote.com/search_results.html?q=daddy&pg=10

www.chicagotribune.com/sports/chi-chicago-fathers-day-sports-photos-photogallery.html

www.countryliving.com/life/g1750/father-day-quotes/

www.deseretnews.com/top/3268/0/Father-is-the-noblest-title-18-quotes-from-LDS-leaders-about-why-dads-matter.html

www.goodhousekeeping.com/holidays/fathers-day/g2419/fathers-day-quotes/

www.goodreads.com/quotes/tag/fathers

www.latina.com/entertainment/celebrity/celebrity-fathers-quotes-advice

www.marieclaire.co.uk/news/celebrity-news/celebrity-dads-best-quotes-on-being-a-father-13726

www.parents.com/parenting/celebrity-parents/celebrity-dad-quotes/

www.quotationspage.com

www.todaysparent.com/blogs/celebrity-candy/celebrity-dad-quotes/

www.whatwillmatter.com/2012/06/quotations-greatest-quotes-about-fathers-and-fatherhood/